CONTENTS

LEFT: **Pink salmon are the most abundant species of salmon in the Great Bear Rainforest. They are counted by the millions as they migrate into the area's many creeks and rivers.**

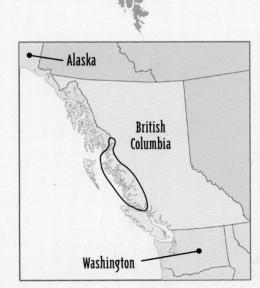

Great Bear Rainforest
British Columbia

Haida
Gwaii

Vancouver
Island

Alaska

British
Columbia

Washington

CHAPTER ONE

A Magical Place

I magine visiting a place where there are trees as tall as skyscrapers, the ocean roars like a lion, and giant bears the color of darkness, snow and gold bullion roam the land like kings. Well, there is such a place. It's on the west coast of British Columbia, and it's called the Great Bear Rainforest.

Reaching from the top of Vancouver Island to the tip of Alaska's Panhandle, and jutting in from the Pacific Ocean to the Coast Mountains, the Great Bear Rainforest is one of the world's last great wildernesses. It's not like a park that you can drive or ride your bike through; it's more like a jungle. A jungle where it rains—and rains and rains—that you can only get to by boat or floatplane. While aboriginal, or First Nations, people have lived in this maze of inlets, bays and fjords for over ten thousand years,

LEFT: **The coastal temperate rainforest is one of the rarest forest types on the planet and also one of the most biologically productive.**

JUST THE BEAR FACTS

What's the weather like in the Great Bear Rainforest?

It's a temperate rainforest, which means it never gets really hot or cold. The mountaintops are always cold, but the forests freeze only in winter, and sometimes not even then. In summer it's warm enough to go outside without a jacket. But it's also very windy, especially near the sea, which is why you often see trees bent over like rickety old men. The rainforest is strongly influenced by the Pacific Ocean, and because the ocean doesn't change temperature very much over the year, neither does the rainforest.

RIGHT: **A rainbow breaks through a midsummer storm on a coastal estuary. Estuaries are where the ocean meets the rainforest; they provide important habitat for coastal bears.**

LEFT: **Springtime in the Great Bear Rainforest. Two subadult grizzly siblings have a wrestling match along a coastal estuary.**

it got its popular name more recently when people concerned about its future set out to tell the world about it. They called it the Great Bear Rainforest because of the great bears that live in it—the grizzly bear, the American black bear and the spirit bear, a rare kind of black bear with white fur. Bears are typically shy of people, but if you're determined to find one, the Great Bear Rainforest is the place to look because thousands of them live there. Most are black bears, but there are hundreds of grizzlies too—great bears that need a great rainforest to survive.

What's surprising is that most of the Great Bear Rainforest isn't a forest at all. Although it covers five million hectares—an area almost as big as the province of Nova Scotia—only a small part is actual rainforest. The rest is made up of steep mountains, windswept glaciers, jagged ice fields and soggy, spongy bogs, all surrounded by a roiling, churning ocean where all sorts of interesting creatures live. If you look at the map on page v, you'll see that the land is so broken up by rivers, streams, fjords,

JUST THE BEAR FACTS

What do scientists learn from studying the Great Bear Rainforest?

There probably isn't a single place on Earth that hasn't been disturbed in some way by humans. But compared to most places, the Great Bear Rainforest is still fairly pristine. That means it's an ideal place for scientists to learn about plants and animals in what is still a relatively natural environment. But even a place as remote as the Great Bear Rainforest is affected by pollution, trophy hunting and habitat destruction. Scientists have discovered, for example, that chemicals banned years ago in North America, but still allowed in Asia, travel to the rainforest in air and marine currents. These chemicals, which are long-lasting and persistent, find their way into the forest's food web. Salmon eat small fish contaminated with them, so they become contaminated too. Then the bears eat the salmon, and they become contaminated. Scientists also have learned that killing large animals like grizzlies for sport can weaken whole populations of bears. They've found that when hunters kill the biggest, strongest bears for trophies, smaller, weaker bears take their places and reproduce. This can result in smaller and weaker populations of bears. Scientists are also studying how the overfishing of salmon affects the rainforest.

inlets and islands that it looks like a giant jigsaw puzzle that someone didn't quite finish fitting together.

But it's in the forests where almost everything lives. There are insects so tiny you need a magnifying glass to see them, grizzlies the size of Volkswagens, and animals of every kind, shape and size in between. In fact, these forests support more living matter, what scientists call *biomass*, than the tropical rainforests in the Amazon. Put another way, even though the Amazon rainforest contains more *different* species, it doesn't have as much living stuff in it overall. No matter where you look in the Great Bear Rainforest—from beneath the forest floor to the tops of the tallest trees—everything is alive. And while a few parts of the Amazon have bears, they aren't like grizzlies. Grizzly bears are only found in northern ecosystems like this one. But just as in the Amazon, everything that lives in the Great Bear Rainforest—plant and animal, large and small—has a vital role to play in it.

The Web of Life

Biologists describe this living world as a "web of life" because all the plants and animals in it depend in some fashion on one another. Each thread in the web represents a kind of plant, insect or animal, so that no matter how small or seemingly insignificant, each and every living thing in the rainforest has an effect on every other living thing. Some plants depend on animals eating parts of them to spread their seeds. Think of birds that eat the fruit off trees,

bushes and vines. Other animals, called carnivores, eat other animals. Think of wolves that catch and kill deer, and eagles, hawks and owls that hunt rabbits and other rodents. Sometimes part of an animal's body will be left uneaten by a predator. When this happens, what's left of it will be eaten by scavengers—everything from gulls to maggots to bacteria. Over time they will break it down into pieces too tiny to see with the naked eye. But even though they're tiny, these microscopic bits have a huge impact on the rainforest because of how they enrich its soil. Think of salmon carcasses that lie along the riverbank after spawning. First birds eat them. Then insects. Then bacteria. But they never really disappear. Instead they fill the soil with nutrients,

TOP: **A rainforest wolf searches for salmon in one of the remote rivers of the Great Bear Rainforest. Wolves feed alongside grizzly and black bears in the fall when the salmon come to spawn. But in the spring and summer these species try to avoid each other.**

JUST THE BEAR FACTS

Is bigger also better?

Not necessarily. Grizzlies may be bigger and stronger than American blacks, but that isn't always an advantage. Yes, grizzlies can scare away smaller, less powerful animals, but they need more food to keep their bigger, more powerful bodies going. That means they have to work harder to find food. It also means if there's less food around for some reason, grizzlies have a tougher time of it than blacks. Compare it to a car. A compact car may not be as fast or powerful as a 500-horsepower muscle car, but the muscle car is going to need a lot more fuel to get around. That's why muscle cars are a lot more expensive to run. It's the same with bears. In nature the rule is that the bigger an animal is, the fewer of them there are. And if you doubt that, think about how many bears there are in the world. Then compare that to how many mice there are.

RIGHT: **There's nothing softer than a mother grizzly bear pillow.**

and it's these nutrients that feed the rainforest plants—everything from the smallest weed to the tallest tree. Just as in a spider's web, every strand in the web of life—in the rainforest—is important. If one or two strands are broken, the web can still hold together. But if too many are cut, it falls apart.

What makes the Great Bear Rainforest so special is that it's an old-growth forest. This means the trees in it have never been logged. In fact, some are over a thousand years old—older than the oldest castles in Europe. They can be as tall as thirty-story buildings and so big around that it would take a dozen people holding hands to form a circle around one. This is exactly the kind of forest bears like.

Rainforest bears rely on the forest for everything. The dens where they spend their winters are usually excavated at the bottoms of sturdy old trees. In the spring and summer they forage for berries and other plants under its broad leafy canopy. And in the fall they feast on the salmon that swim through its streams to spawn. The forest filters the rain that falls through it day after day, so the temperature for spawning is just right. And no matter the season, bears rely on the forest's thick tangle of bushes, shrubs and trees for protection. That's why when old-growth forests disappear, grizzlies disappear too. It's one of the reasons why you have to go so far north in British Columbia to find significant populations of them.

But the forest isn't just a place for bears. People have lived in the Great Bear Rainforest for a long time too. If you travel to any of the First Nations communities on the coast, you'll find likenesses of bears carved

JUST THE BEAR FACTS

What kinds of trees are found in the Great Bear Rainforest?

Mainly Sitka spruce, western red cedar, western hemlock and shore pine. All these trees have cones and needles instead of leaves, and stay green year round. There are also some deciduous trees. These are trees that lose their leaves in winter and grow them back in spring. They include the red alder, black cottonwood, vine maple and a variety of willows.

RIGHT: **Mother grizzly and her first-year cub search for salmon eggs buried in a dried-out river bed. Grizzly bears have big muscles and have no problem rolling over large rocks in search of food.**

LEFT: **Heiltsuk First Nation grizzly bear mask.**

on the corner posts of the big houses where dances and festivals are held. You'll also find masks and other works of art that celebrate the bear as something to revere and respect. Coastal First Nations people have lived alongside the great bears for thousands of years and know them better than anyone else. So they have much to teach the rest of the world about them.

More recently, the rainforest has become a destination for tourists. Visitors come to witness the wildness of the place and for the chance to see the rare and precious white spirit bear. But it isn't easy to get into the rainforest because it's so remote. Hardly any roads lead to it. That's why if you do manage to get there, you'll find that a boat is the best way to get around. But most important, if you are fortunate enough to visit one day, remember to bring rain gear. They don't call it a rainforest for nothing. In the wettest parts it can rain as much as five meters (more than fifteen feet) a year. That's the equivalent of a two-story house. But without that much rain, there would be no Great Bear Rainforest. And without the Great Bear Rainforest, there would be no great bears.

JUST THE BEAR FACTS

Do people live in the Great Bear Rainforest?

Absolutely. Culturally, it's one of the richest places on Earth, though communities in it tend to be small and far apart. There are only a few towns like Bella Coola, Kitimat and Prince Rupert that have roads and populations anywhere near 25,000 people. Most communities are much smaller and located in remote reaches of the rainforest. Villages like Klemtu, Bella Bella, Hartley Bay and Rivers Inlet are located on or near First Nations ancestral village sites that are thousands of years old. Included among the coastal First Nations are the Coast Tsimshian, Gwa'Sala, Haisla, Heiltsuk, Henaaksiala, Kitasoo-Xaixais, Kwakwaka'wakw, Nisga'a, Nuxalk, and Oweekeno peoples. In earlier times, these nations had many more villages, though some were used only seasonally. For example, a village site on the outer coast may have been used in the summer as a place for people to harvest shellfish and other seafood when the ocean was calm. It is only recently that First Nations have moved into more permanent communities.

RIGHT: **Young grizzly bears—called subadults—come in many colors, ranging from black to blond, but most are a rich chocolate brown like this one.**

CHAPTER TWO

Winter

If you're a bear in the Great Bear Rainforest, life usually begins in December or January because that's when cubs are born. Rainforest bears spend almost two-thirds of the year feeding themselves so that when they go back to their dens in late November or early December, they will have enough fat on them to survive until the following spring. That's even more important if you're a female bear about to have cubs, because your cubs will rely on the rich, fatty milk you produce for all their nourishment. Newborn bears aren't much bigger than puppies when they appear in the cozy dry warmth of their mother's den, but thanks to their mother's milk, they grow fast. By the time they take their first sniff of fresh mountain air in early March or April, they're already as big as footballs.

LEFT: **A mother grizzly and her three cubs explore a beach at low tide. These cubs left their winter den only four months earlier, but they have already learned how to swim and dig for clams. Soon they will learn to catch salmon.**

JUST THE BEAR FACTS

How does hibernation differ from sleep?

When an animal is asleep, it moves regularly, has an active brain and can wake up quickly. When an animal is hibernating, its body functions slow down dramatically. It doesn't move and it takes a long time to wake up and move around. True hibernators include bats, chipmunks, dormice, ground squirrels, hamsters, raccoons, skunks and marmots. Whether bears are true hibernators is still a subject of debate.

RIGHT: **A grizzly cub with gravel on his nose helps his mother dig up fatty salmon eggs that have been laid in the spawning beds.**

Most of the time bears like to return to the same dens year after year, though sometimes they build new ones. Often these dens are dug under the roots of old-growth trees and are about the size of a Smart Car, just big enough to house a mother bear with two to three cubs. The tree's roots help anchor the earth so it's easier for the bears to dig around them, and they protect the finished dens from winter avalanches. But unlike a Smart Car, bear dens don't have windows, only a door covered with several meters of snow in winter. The snow insulates the den and makes it a warm and inviting place for a bear to sleep.

Adult bears living on the British Columbia coast spend most of the winter in their dens. They do get up now and then to stretch and keep their muscles active, and sometimes as spring approaches they even go outside for a short look around. Cubs also have to wake up sometimes and move around to feed. But it's not until March, when the heavy snow starts to melt and the first hints of spring fill the air, that it's finally time for them to go outside for good. Mothers always go first. They look in every direction to make sure it's safe. Then the cubs follow, and for the first time in their lives they get to see the vast wilderness that will be their home.

Later on in summer, plants in the Great Bear Rainforest grow so tall and thick that if you manage to break your way through them, they'll fold up behind you as if you were never there. But in winter it's different. Most of the shrubs have died back almost to nothing, and you can see some distance in almost every direction. Young bears getting their first taste

of the rainforest will stick their noses into everything and romp and play like children in a playground. But they never wander far from their mothers, because even though it might look as if they're playing, they're really learning. During the three years grizzly cubs spend with their mothers, they take in everything she shows them. They learn what to eat, where to find it, what to be careful of and what to be scared of.

March is an unpredictable month in the rainforest. Sometimes it can be sunny and warm, and sometimes it can be cold, wet and windy. Sometimes a late snow will turn it white. When storms rush in from the Pacific or roar down from the mountains, the wind blows so hard that trees can break in half. It's also so loud that sometimes bears can't hear each other or anything else. But who needs sensitive ears when you have a world-class nose? Bears' noses are so powerful they can smell food—or each other—kilometers away. Good thing too, because life can be dangerous for young bears. Even grizzlies. A grizzly cub can be attacked by cougars, wolves and even adult male grizzlies. This is why grizzly mothers always try to keep their cubs as far away from other bears as they can.

Finding food can be tricky too. In the early spring there's not much to eat except for a few plants that have begun to sprout on the rainforest floor. But until the salmon start to run in fall, all rainforest bears, even grizzlies, depend on plants for almost all their nourishment. So the sooner they can find some to eat, the better. If you're a bear, the warmer, more productive days of April and May can't come quickly enough.

JUST THE BEAR FACTS

Why are grizzlies shaped the way they are?

Grizzlies have powerful shoulders and long sharp claws to dig roots and bulbs out of the ground. These mighty shoulders make them look as if they have a hump on their backs. This hump is one of the features that distinguishes them from black bears, who don't have such powerful shoulders. When grizzlies dig out a piece of ground, it looks as if it's been gone over with a rototiller.

LEFT: **A mother grizzly will spend three years with her cub exploring the rainforest and teaching a variety of life lessons, such as where the tastiest plants and best fishing spots are.**

JUST THE BEAR FACTS

Are bears true hibernators?

No one can say for sure, though more and more scientists believe they aren't. When they go to their dens to sleep, they use up almost half the fat they stored the previous year. This means they can go months without eating, drinking, urinating or defecating (although mother bears will eat the waste from their cubs. Yuck!). However, unlike true hibernators, bears may leave their dens occasionally. In the Great Bear Rainforest, they may come out if food—like a really late run of salmon—is suddenly available. Because of this and the fact that their body temperatures don't drop as low as those of true hibernators, like bats, there is some doubt as to whether bears really do hibernate. It could simply be a long winter's nap.

RIGHT: **A coastal black bear stands among the remains of salmon that have spawned and died. Thanks to all the fish this bear has successfully caught and eaten, he should enjoy a nice long winter's sleep.**

CHAPTER THREE

Spring

Visit the Great Bear Rainforest in spring and you'll find a place buzzing with new life. Throughout April, May and June, it's like a baby-animal factory. Sitka black-tailed deer have fawns. Wolf packs have pups. Killer whale pods have calves. Eagles have chicks. And on it goes.

The plant kingdom is bursting with life too. Deciduous trees grow leaves that reach out like tiny fingers from branches that were once bare, while coniferous, or evergreen, trees, tired of their dowdy winter look, grow fresh, light green shoots all over. Smaller plants become active too. As the sun gets warmer and rises higher in the sky, plants that spent the winter hiding underground begin to shoot through, reaching for the precious rays of light that filter through the trees.

LEFT: **After polar bears, grizzlies have the second-slowest reproduction cycle of animals in North America. This is one of the reasons grizzly mothers are so protective of their cubs.**

JUST THE BEAR FACTS

How big is a rainforest bear?

American black bears are considered medium-sized bears, meaning they weigh anywhere from 60 to 300 kilograms (130 to 660 pounds). A really, really big male grizzly bear can weigh 600 kilograms (1,300 pounds) and stand more than 3 meters (10 feet) tall on his hind legs. Females are about two-thirds that size.

RIGHT: **Salmon blood stains the white fur of this spirit or Kermode bear. These rare and beautiful white bears of the rainforest were once thought by early European settlers to be polar bears who had lost their way.**

LEFT: **Bunchberry, one of the many plants that are found throughout the rainforest.**

The unending miracle of life is never more miraculous than in spring, when everything—plant and animal—is busy renewing itself.

In late March and early April it's still cool in the rainforest. The days are getting longer, but it will be a while yet before the sun starts to beat down on the forest with any real strength. So it also will be a while before the forest floor fills up with the many different kinds of plants that bears depend on for food. But that doesn't matter. After their long winter rest, bears are slow starters. They don't rush around like spring colts shaking off winter blahs. Cubs are always excited to be outside for the first time, and, like youngsters of any kind, they will use up a lot of energy charging around. But adults move slower. When it comes to finding food, they're happy to make do with whatever plants are at hand. And in early spring what's at hand—

JUST THE BEAR FACTS

What are some of the grizzly bear's favorite plants?

Angelica, Lyngby's and other sedges, Douglas' water hemlock, red-osier dogwood, horsetail, cow parsnip, black twinberry, Nootka lupine, silverweed, rice root, skunk cabbage, devil's club, mountain sweet cicely, stink currant, thimbleberry, salmonberry, red elderberry, small-flowered bulrush, twisted stalk, blueberries and red huckleberries, false hellebore and highbush cranberry.

or paw—is primarily skunk cabbage, named for the pungent odor it emits—an odor that attracts pollinating bees and flies. So if your eyes don't recognize the bright green and yellow cabbage-like plant poking out of the moist ground at your feet, your nose sure will. And if you can smell a skunk cabbage with your relatively weak nose, think how tempting the smell must be for bears with their rocket-powered snouts.

In southern British Columbia, snowdrops and crocuses herald the spring. Up north it's skunk cabbage, because it actually generates heat that melts snow. How's that for a force of nature? And instead of petals, it grows a single hood-shaped, leaf-like sheath called a *spathe*. But for bears the only part of a skunk cabbage that holds any interest is the roots. Why? Because they're the most nutritious part, so they're

RIGHT: A mother grizzly enjoys a meal of sedges by the water's edge. Lyngby's sedge, a favorite of coastal bears, is found only in intertidal zones or along the ocean shoreline. During the spring and early summer, this is one of the most important food sources for coastal bears because of its high crude protein content.

LEFT: Grizzly and black bears love to eat skunk cabbage. When the bears dig up the root of the cabbage, they leave little holes in the ground, which trap water during dry times and help ensure the growth of next year's crop.

the only part bears actually eat. It's one of the first lessons newborn cubs learn from their mothers.

Bears dig hundreds of skunk cabbages out of the earth when they're hungry. When they're finished, the ground looks as if a crew of really bad golfers has hacked away at it with pitching wedges. But the holes they leave also become places where new cabbages grow. This is typical of how the rainforest works. Even though it may not look like it sometimes, everything contributes to the growth and spread of everything else. The web of life.

Later, as the sun grows stronger and the days get longer, other kinds of roots and shoots sprout too, and what were once patches of lifeless brown earth become gardens of newly minted green. More than two hundred different kinds of plants grow in the Great Bear Rainforest, and bears enjoy a good many of them. By late April the sun has started to hit the forest's many estuaries (places where rivers and streams flow out to sea), which is where sedges grow.

JUST THE BEAR FACTS

How fast can bears run?

Because grizzlies have no natural enemies other than humans, and very rarely have to chase after prey the way wolves do, being able to run fast isn't as important to them as it is for other animals. Even so, they can run as fast as 50 kilometers (30 miles) per hour for a kilometer or two. Black bears can run even faster—up to 60 kph. They're also very good at climbing trees. They wrap their front paws around a trunk and hoist themselves up using their hind legs. Grizzly bears can climb trees too, but they do it far less often than black bears. Some observers say they're not as good at it as black bears. No wonder. Black bears often have to climb trees to escape predators. Grizzlies don't. Grizzlies are also heavier, and it's more difficult to climb a tree when you're big.

LEFT: **When clamming, some bears eat everything—shell and all. Others will open up the shell and eat only the meat inside.**

RIGHT: **Bears don't run very often, but when they do they can run as fast as a horse—though only for a short distance.**

JUST THE BEAR FACTS

When are bears most active?

It was once thought that bears only came out at night. Now scientists know they can be out and about at all times of the day. When they're most active—whether at night, during the day or in between—is now thought to depend on the time of year and the available food supply. In the Great Bear Rainforest, black bears spend more time out at night than grizzlies do because it's safer for them.

RIGHT: **While this bear looks like it is drinking from the salty ocean, it is actually drinking just the surface water, which is mostly fresh.**

LEFT: **Grizzly bears are excellent swimmers and sometimes enjoy playing in the water, especially on hot summer days when they need to cool off.**

Sedges are grass-like plants that can tolerate both fresh and salt water. They can grow over two meters (six feet) tall if the bears don't get them first. In a way, estuaries are the closest thing the rainforest has to pastures in that they're places where bears can graze on sedges the way bison graze on prairie grass.

Because estuaries are close to the shoreline, there are vast helpings of seafood to be had near them as well. If you've ever tried prying a barnacle off a rock, you'll know it isn't easy. But for a bear it's like cracking open a soda. They eat barnacles the way people eat popcorn. And when they flip rocks over, they set free dozens of small crabs and eels underneath. Then they chase them like hockey players going after a puck.

During their first year out, cubs depend on their mother's milk for all their food; they won't eat what she eats until the following year. Their teeth aren't strong enough to bite into something like a barnacle, and they need the fat they can only get from suckling

JUST THE BEAR FACTS

What happens when grizzlies run into humans?

It's so rare for a grizzly to attack a human that when it does happen it makes front-page news. But it's not rare for humans to attack grizzlies. Every year the British Columbian government allows hundreds of grizzlies and thousands of black bears to be killed for sport. And many more are shot at or near landfills or garbage dumps by conservation officers. Because of this, and because no one has figured out a way to accurately count the number of bears in BC, no one knows how many grizzlies are left in the Great Bear Rainforest and elsewhere in the province. The government says there could be as many as 17,000 grizzlies in the whole of British Columbia, but scientists and conservationists say there are far fewer.

their mothers. But just because they're not old enough to enjoy a fresh crab dinner doesn't mean they don't like a game. So like their mother, who not only chases after sea creatures but also fills her stomach with them, cubs go after sea critters too. Sometimes they get so carried away that they tumble headfirst into the ocean. But scary as this might be for them, it's usually nothing to worry about. Bears are like boats. When you toss them in water, they float. So who needs swimming lessons?

And through it all, the rain will fall. There may be days when it's dry and even kind of summery. Those are the most comfortable days for people. But bears don't care either way—in fact, they seem to prefer the rain. Even in the spring, the sun can be too hot for a bear with a thick fur coat. So while we probably would scurry under a tree when the clouds open and the curtains of rain start to close, bears just carry on. Wet or dry, it makes little difference to them.

As spring sets in and the snow begins to disappear, bears also may find a dead animal carcass to eat—perhaps a moose or mountain goat, crushed in a winter avalanche. That may not sound very appetizing to you, but to a bear family it's treasure—like discovering a freezer full of food. However, treasure has a way of attracting pirates, and after a long winter, many of the coast's other predators are hungry too. So if a mother bear and her cubs find a dead moose, it may not be long before a pack of wolves picks up the scent as well. Then they'll move in like ants at a picnic. Except it's no picnic for the bears. It doesn't matter that bears are much bigger

than wolves. A bear on its own—even a full-sized bear, let alone a cub—is no match for a wolf pack. Wolves have been known to drive bears up trees and wait hours for them to come down. When they do, they're usually so tired from clinging to the tree top that they don't have a chance against the pack. So you can bet that when wolves are around, a mother bear—even a mother grizzly—with cubs to protect will get well out of their way.

Young British Columbian grizzlies usually stay with their mothers for three full years before they strike out on their own, and a pair of grizzly cubs might roam together for another year after that. Black and spirit bear cubs stay with their moms half as long, but the time they spend with their mothers

TOP: **A family of grizzly bears explores its lush home. The vegetation in the rainforest grows so thick that coastal bears are rarely seen in spring and summer.**

is just as important. It's also the only time in a bear's life when he or she will have other bears for company. Eventually all bears—blacks and grizzlies, males and females—leave their families to live alone. That's why if you come across a bear in the wilderness, he or she will almost always be on his or her own. Unlike wolves, who live in extended families or packs, or birds that flock together for protection, adult bears don't need other bears to survive. The only times they come together are when they mate in May and June, and during the fall when they gather along the banks of rivers to fish. Sometimes two bears will pass each other on their way from one place to another, but that's the extent of their socializing. An adult male grizzly can live more than thirty years, and he'll spend most of those years by himself.

Male bears let other bears know what piece of the rainforest belongs to them by marking their borders with pee, and scratching and rubbing their scent into trees and tracks in the ground. Throughout the rainforest, certain trees are used year after year as "mark" trees. These trees are usually spruce or amabilis fir. Both ooze with sticky sap. The bears rub their scent into the sap and then move on to the next "marked" tree. This way they can keep track of each other in the river valley without having to bump into other bears. It's like a hotel registry, and everyone has to sign in.

Grizzly bear paw prints can be big—as big as dinner plates. If you came across a set and didn't know better, you might think they were Sasquatch tracks. A male grizzly's territory can encompass hundreds of square kilometers—the equivalent of multiple river valleys—because it takes that much land to feed him.

JUST THE BEAR FACTS

How widespread are American black bears and grizzlies?

American blacks are the most common bear in the rainforest and the most common bear in the whole world, with a range extending from Alaska through mainland Canada and Newfoundland to the eastern United States. Grizzlies are far less common. Their range extends from Alaska through British Columbia and parts of Alberta to Idaho, Wyoming and Montana in the northern US. But no farther. Once upon a time they could be found as far south as California and Mexico. In fact, there is still a picture of a grizzly bear on the California state flag. But throughout the late nineteenth and early twentieth centuries, grizzlies were wiped out of most of North America. That's why it's so important that we preserve what little of the continent is still left to them.

LEFT: **Small flies surround a grizzly as it feeds on a variety of rainforest plants. During the spring and summer, bears will eat dozens of different plant species, but once fall comes they switch almost entirely to salmon.**

33

JUST THE BEAR FACTS

What kinds of animals live in the Great Bear Rainforest?

As well as bears, more than 230 species of birds and 68 mammals live in the rainforest, not to mention dozens of reptiles and amphibians, and hundreds of different sorts of insects. Some of the best-known and most recognizable animals are the cougar, gray wolf, Sitka black-tailed deer, hoary marmot, pine marten, mountain goat, bald eagle, Canada goose, harbor seal, Steller's sea lion, elephant seal, river otter, puffin, sea gull, gray whale, humpback whale, killer whale, and Pacific white-sided dolphin.

Mothers with cubs have much smaller ranges. It's safer for them that way because the more they explore, the more dangers they may encounter. Their best strategy is to not move about too much. Black bears have the smallest territories of all.

But if bears go out of their way to avoid other bears, they certainly see lots of other rainforest animals. Picture it: Above them, eagles and great blue herons build nests. Insects parade up and down trees like soldiers. Beavers smack their paddle tails on pond surfaces. Porcupines hang from tree branches, while pine martens, always on the lookout for a meal, chase gray squirrels. Along the seashore, gulls crack open crabs, and mink break open duck eggs. Ravens screech in the sky, and up on a craggy bluff a mountain goat clings to the steep rock like a climber on K2. This is what scientists mean by "the teeming rainforest." It's a place where something is going on all the time, even if our sometimes lazy eyes fail to see it.

RIGHT: **A spirit bear shows the results of a recent mud bath. There are only about 400 such bears in the whole Great Bear Rainforest, making them one of the rarest animals on earth.**

LEFT: **Porcupines are sometimes described as looking like little bears. These prickly animals are just one of the many species that live in the rainforest.**

CHAPTER FOUR

Summer

Ah, summer. In the Great Bear Rainforest it's as changeable as the wind. In a good year the rain will let up somewhat, and there will be days—maybe even weeks—when the gray sky turns blue. In a bad year it will rain so hard you'd think someone had turned on a heavenly tap. It's impossible to predict. It never gets really hot in the rainforest, but on warm, dry days in July and August you can wander around in shorts and a T-shirt and feel fine. Not only that, you can wander around in daylight from early morning to late at night. Because the Great Bear Rainforest is so far north, the midsummer sun rises before 4:00 AM and sets after 11:00 PM. And when it does get dark, it does so halfheartedly, as if the sky can't make up its mind.

If you did wander around, you'd better watch your step because the rainforest is an unpredictable,

LEFT: **The bright purple Nootka lupine, another favorite bear food, is found along the banks of Great Bear Rainforest rivers and estuaries.**

JUST THE BEAR FACTS

Do bears ever stand up?

Occasionally a bear will stand up and walk on his or her hind legs like a person. But they don't do it for long, and when they do it's usually to get a better look around or to sniff the air for possible intruders. They also may stand up if they want to lean against a tree and rub their backs. Aaaaah, that feels good.

RIGHT: **Mother and cub, up to their shoulders in delicious sedges. This salt-water-tolerant plant can grow over two meters (six feet) tall and will be taller than even the largest bears by the end of summer.**

LEFT: **Over 100 of the rivers in the Great Bear Rainforest are still untouched by logging and industry, and so provide some of the best bear habitat in the world.**

even dangerous, place. There are no human-made trails in it the way there are in a park. It's not a place where the roses are here and the tulips there. In the rainforest everything grows everywhere. There are no empty spaces. That's because no matter what the space is like—smooth, rough, sandy or peaty—something will grow on it. And summer is when plants grow like crazy—so fast it seems as if you can watch them grow. It's a time when even a family of bears may have to think twice about whether to zig or zag or turn around and go back the way they came.

In summer there are so many plants in the rainforest, and they grow so fast and dense, that no sooner do you break your way through a wall of salmonberry or salal bushes than they'll close up behind you as if you'd never been there. Devil's club, a plant with a cone-shaped cluster of flowers and painfully sharp spines, which is found only in Pacific rainforests like the Great Bear, grows so tall that even grizzlies have to look up to see the top of it. And summer is when it grows to devilish proportions.

And yet, if there is a time when life in the rainforest gets easy, it's summer. With food of every kind so plentiful, finding it isn't the hard slog it is during the rest of the year, especially in winter. We know bears sleep during the winter, but for other rainforest animals like wolves and deer, winter can be a desperate time as they search, often in vain, for a meal. Not in summer. When everything is tall and green and full of life, there's always something for the forest's plant eaters to chew on. And after a long, hard winter they often have a lot of chewing to do. Meat eaters, or carnivores, like wolves, also have more choice because there are more small animals around—animals like mice, voles and marmots, who spend winter hibernating underground.

Late May and early June are also when the bears of the Great Bear Rainforest mate. When they're ready, males will secrete natural chemicals from their bodies into the sap of the "mark" trees for females to recognize and respond to. You could call it advertising, and what they're advertising is themselves. The biggest, strongest, most powerful males get the greatest number of mates. Unlike some animals, such as eagles, who find one mate to share their lives with, male bears will mate with as many females as they can, both in a single season and throughout their lives. By doing this, they better their chances of ensuring that their genes will be carried into the future by cubs.

By mid-June most female bears that already have cubs and therefore aren't interested in mating will have done their best to find prime feeding spots.

JUST THE BEAR FACTS

What's dangerous to a bear?

Bears, especially bear cubs, can be attacked by wolves, cougars and other larger bears. A large male grizzly will sometimes kill a female's cubs so she will mate with him and have his cubs instead. But the main dangers bears face are from people. Sport hunters kill them legally and poachers kill them illegally, often for their organs, which are used in traditional Asian medicine. Conservation officers will also kill them if they get into landfill sites or people's garbage. That's why more and more small towns in British Columbia are making it mandatory for people to bear-proof their garbage. They don't want bears coming into town to disturb and frighten the people who live there, and, just as important, they don't want to have to kill bears who have grown accustomed to eating food they find in garbage cans or at campsites.

LEFT: **A tree-hugging bear rubs his scent into this Sitka spruce. These scent or "mark" trees are used by bears to keep tabs on each other in the rainforest. All a bear has to do is smell the tree and he or she can identify other bears who have also signed in there.**

Among the places they like best are avalanche chutes. These are tracks along mountainsides where avalanches routinely fall, so there are few, if any, tall trees in them. This absence of trees means the sun reaches these chutes before it strikes anywhere else in the forest, so plants grow faster than in places where it's shady. Unlike people, bears don't need to be told to eat their greens, and many of their favorite greens grow in avalanche chutes. As well, these chutes may be close to the sea, so it's easy for bears to get from them to the beach and all the delicious sea creatures that live along the shore. Chutes also provide perfect places to nap, which bears enjoy doing when it gets hot. These napping spots, which are usually no more than shallow beds dug in the ground, are high up, so when the bears wake they have a clear view of every-thing around them. That way they can hear anyone or anything that might be coming their way. This makes them feel safe. And it allows the bears to keep from tripping over each other in the same rainforest berry patch.

Speaking of berries, bears are nuts about them. They like nothing better than to plunk down in the middle of a thick bramble and chow on the juicy ripe berries that grow there. And summer is when berries are their sweetest and tastiest. Devil's club berries, elderberries, twinberries, salmonberries, huckle-berries, blueberries, thimbleberries, salal berries, gooseberries and saskatoons: if it's a berry, a bear will eat it. When you're as big as a bear, you have to eat all the time to maintain your size and strength, so bears can spend twenty out of every twenty-four

JUST THE BEAR FACTS

Why are there so few grizzlies?
For every grizzly in BC, there are probably ten or twenty black bears. Why? There are three reasons. First, grizzlies need much bigger territories than blacks because they're bigger bears. Remember, the bigger you are, the more fuel you need to get around. Second, blacks are more tolerant of people so they can live in places where humans live too. Grizzlies aren't like that. Despite their reputation for being ferocious, what they really want is to be left alone. And third, grizzlies reproduce very slowly. They have the second-slowest reproduction cycle of any land mammal in North America; only the polar bear reproduces more slowly. A female grizzly must be at least five years old before she has her first set of cubs, and after that she'll only get pregnant once every three years. A black bear can have cubs every other year. And even if a female grizzly does manage to produce two or three cubs every three years, there's no guarantee that those cubs will live to be adults.

LEFT: **A mother grizzly and cub share a quiet moment together before they move down to the river to begin fishing for salmon.**

JUST THE BEAR FACTS

What's a bog?

These are places made of springy, spongy material called *peat*. There's very little soil in a bog, so the trees in them are dwarfed. A three-hundred-year-old cedar that would stand 20 or 30 meters (65 or 100 feet) tall somewhere else might be no bigger than an average-sized man in a bog. Bogs are also very wet, so they're tricky to walk on. If you don't watch your step, you could sink up to your hips. It's only during the winter, when the bogs freeze, that walking on them is easy.

RIGHT: **These two-year-old grizzly cubs will spend another full year with their mother before they set off to start their own families.**

hours doing nothing but stuffing their faces. You've probably heard the expression "hungry as a bear"; now you know where it comes from. What makes things tricky is that not everything's ready to eat at the same time. Salmonberries ripen in June, thimbleberries in July, huckleberries in August and rosehips in September. So cubs have to watch their mothers closely to learn when to eat as well as what and how.

Bears also dig up the ground to get at roots, tubers and bulbs. But just as they do with berries, they eat different roots at different times. Why? Think of carrots. Baby ones may be sweet and tender when they start growing in spring, but if you wait till the end of summer when they're full size, they'll be that much bigger and more nourishing.

Bears also need protein, and while grizzlies are certainly strong enough to kill a deer, insects are much easier prey. For bears, the ants and termites they find when they overturn a log or tree stump are a feast. Because, don't forget, turning over a log is no trouble for a bear. They can push a log over as easily as people can fall off one. Coastal bears also love beetle larvae, bees and wasps. After all, what are a few pesky stings to a grizzly? And like people, they like honey. It's sweet, gooey and full of good stuff to grow on.

Sometimes mother bears want their cubs out of the way so they can go off and feed by themselves. But how and where do you store two or three young cubs safely for a few hours? Up a tree, that's where. Imagine looking up and seeing a family of bear cubs, none of them bigger than a round-eared, long-snouted dog, staring back at you. And when their mother

tells them to stay put, they stay put. Unlike human children, they won't sneak back to the ground just to see if they can.

However, even though sending cubs up a tree is supposed to keep them safe, it can have the opposite effect. Hunters aren't allowed to kill mother bears with cubs, but if the mother is seen to be alone while her cubs are up a tree, a hunter would have no way of knowing she has cubs. So he might go ahead and kill her anyway. This is one reason so many bear cubs are orphaned each year. And an orphaned bear cub can't survive without his or her mother.

Meanwhile, at the seashore, rainforest bears never know when they'll run across a beached gray whale or an elephant seal to take a bite out of. That's why the beach is like a big banquet table for them. Except, unlike a lot of people, bears don't care for sunbathing. Would you if you wore a fur coat all the time? That's why in the summer the best time to see bears is when the tide is out, either early in the morning or when the sun is ready to set. Then it's cool and damp—perfect bear weather. Picture it: a shoreline bathed in cool gray mist, green trees, reddish seaweed, black rocks, a silver sea and a family of clam-digging, crab-grabbing, rock-flipping, beachcombing bears.

JUST THE BEAR FACTS

How do bears go to the bathroom when they sleep?

Unlike other animals that hibernate during the winter, bears don't get rid of their body wastes when they sleep. Instead, waste products are broken down by their kidneys and liver and turned into proteins.

LEFT: **This five-year-old spirit bear lives on an island in the middle of the Great Bear Rainforest and each summer patiently awaits the return of pink salmon.**

JUST THE BEAR FACTS

How do you get to see a grizzly?

Because grizzlies live in such remote parts of British Columbia, seeing one isn't easy. But more and more people are getting the chance thanks to tour operators who specialize in taking ecotourists to places where grizzlies live. The easiest and safest way to see a live grizzly bear is by boat. Tour operators organize cruises to different parts of the Great Bear Rainforest where they know grizzlies gather, usually at the mouths of rivers. Grizzly watching is becoming a more and more important part of the coastal economy, and as long as it's done carefully, it can help protect bears because it proves that, in financial terms, a live bear is many times more valuable than a dead one.

RIGHT: **Grizzly bear siblings sporting luxuriant coats. As these two bears get older, they will lose their bright blond highlights and become darker in color.**

CHAPTER FIVE

Fall

Like all British Columbian forests, the Great Bear Rainforest is composed mainly of evergreen trees that remain green all winter long. But remember there are deciduous trees too. In September, when the days get shorter and the air grows cooler, the leaves on these once-green trees turn russet and gold. If you're lucky enough to visit the forest on a dry fall day when the sun is out, the sky is blue and the trees above you have knitted together a green, scarlet and yellow quilt, you will see one of the most beautiful scenes in nature. One of these trees, the Pacific crab apple, is a fall favorite of coastal bears, and the sight of a chocolate brown bear standing on his hind legs as he reaches for the tree's crimson fruit is one you'll never forget.

LEFT: **In the fall, grizzly bears wait eagerly for the return of salmon, their favorite food. But they also enjoy the small crimson fruit of the Pacific crab apple tree.**

JUST THE BEAR FACTS

How much salmon does a single bear eat?

This, of course, depends on the individual bear, but one study of black bears on Haida Gwaii, formerly known as the Queen Charlotte Islands, showed they ate as many as 12 fish a day during a 45-day period in the fall. An average coastal bear will consume about 20,000 calories a day when he or she is preparing for winter. That's the equivalent of more than 40 Big Macs.

RIGHT: **This grizzly has caught a large chum salmon for lunch. Chum or "dog" salmon are especially fat and much sought after by hungry bears like this one.**

LEFT: **Spawned-out pink salmon like these will be eaten by many different scavengers, although, given a choice, bears prefer fresh salmon. Grizzly bears are just one of nearly 200 species of rainforest creatures that are known to depend on salmon as a food source.**

But it's not just crab apples that tell rainforest bears it's fall. There's something indefinable in the air that lets them—and their noses—know it's time to leave their summer berry patches behind and head to the nearest river. That's because fall is when salmon return to the rainforest's rivers and streams to spawn, and bears' noses are so powerful and sensitive they can smell the salmon even when they're still at sea. It's a smell bears love! They can't wait for the large silvery fish to come back to the rainforest, because they know that once they do, everything about their own lives will change.

Scientists describe salmon as a "foundation" species. That may sound like a strange thing to say, but just as a building has a foundation, so, in a way, has the rainforest, and the salmon are it. What this means is that the survival of many rainforest species,

including bears, depends in a big way on them. Their life cycle begins in the spring when millions upon millions of young salmon swim downstream and out to the open ocean. How far they travel and where they go is still a mystery. Depending on what kind of salmon they are, they'll remain at sea for two and a half to four and a half years. That is, if they aren't caught and eaten by a killer whale, a sea lion, a seal or a human being first. However, when those years are up and fall comes, they find their way back to the very river where they were born and the exact place where they hatched.

The journey up the home river is often a tremendously difficult one made against a swift and merciless current. You may have seen pictures of salmon jumping waterfalls from one pool to another. Think of the strength and determination it takes to do that. And they don't always succeed. They may have to try several times before they manage a leap like that, only to have to do it all over again a little farther up the river. But the salmon keep pushing because they know somehow that it's the only way they're going to get a chance to lay their eggs and make sure future generations follow them. That relentless drive to reproduce is true for all life on Earth. No matter what you are—plant or animal—you always want to make sure that others like you follow in your place.

The rainforest salmon run is one of the most amazing migrations on Earth, and just how they manage it year after year is still something that puzzles scientists. Some researchers think it has to do with the way a particular river smells. Others suggest the fish

JUST THE BEAR FACTS

How do bears choose the salmon they eat?

According to a study done in Alaska, when there are lots of fish to choose from, bears tend to be fussy. Instead of eating just any old fish, they will search for the most energy-rich ones—that is, those that have not yet spawned. And when they eat those salmon, they tend to focus on the parts that contain the most nutrients—eggs in females and brains in males. However, when salmon aren't quite so abundant, bears will eat just about anything, and they won't waste any of the fish.

LEFT: **Coastal bears spend a great deal of time in the water. In their search for sedge-filled estuaries and the best salmon runs, they regularly must cross fjords, inlets, rivers and streams. Of course, they also like to cool off when the weather gets warm.**

JUST THE BEAR FACTS

Are spirit bears protected from hunting?

Yes, it is illegal to kill a spirit bear. But it's not illegal to hunt black bears, even though many black bears carry the spirit bear's recessive gene—that is, the gene that turns it white. This means a hunter may kill a black bear that could have given birth to a spirit bear.

RIGHT: **Sockeye salmon like these ones turn bright red when they enter their fresh-water spawning grounds. Sockeye are very specialized salmon and can only spawn near large lake systems. Unlike pink or chum salmon, sockeye do not head right out into the ocean after they are born, but prefer to stay in the fresh-water environment for up to two years. The rich, dark red meat of the sockeye is prized by both humans and bears.**

have some sort of compass system built into them. Whatever the secret, it's a true biological miracle.

When they finally do come upon the spot where they were born, female salmon look for a gravelly bed to lay their eggs. Each one lays thousands of them. Nature seems to know that only a few of the tiny salmon that hatch from these thousands of original eggs will survive long enough to become adult salmon and swim back up the river to reproduce. The rest will die as young fish on their way to sea, as adult fish swimming in the ocean, or as spent fish on their way home up rivers, where they are caught by hungry rainforest animals like bears.

As salmon migrate from the ocean to fresh water, they begin to change color and shape as they prepare to spawn. The color they turn depends on what kind of salmon they are. Pink and chum salmon turn mottled shades of black and white, while coho and sockeye turn red. Pink salmon develop humps on their backs, which is why they're sometimes called "humpies." Chums, which develop larger curved jaws, are called "dogs." Chinook turn a mottled red and are known as "springs," "kings" or, if they're really big, "tyees."

Once a female salmon lays her eggs, a male will fertilize them and help cover them with gravel. Then the two salmon, mom and dad, will stand ready to protect the eggs from other salmon that may try to use the same spot. This completes the spawning process. Then, their journey over and their work done, the male and female die, and the cycle of life they began when they hatched in the same riverbed two or three or four years earlier is complete. The following

spring, the eggs the female laid and both parents guarded in the fall will hatch, and the miraculous salmon cycle will begin all over again.

Without the salmon, which feed not only bears but also wolves, otters, eagles and more than two hundred other species of rainforest animals, the Great Bear Rainforest would be a very different place. But vital as the salmon are, their annual return is no sure thing. Sometimes disaster strikes and they don't come back.

This happened recently in a place called the Broughton Archipelago, on the southern edge of the Great Bear Rainforest. Millions of pink salmon were expected to turn up at the end of summer to swim upstream, spawn and die as they had for thousands of years. Instead, only a few thousand appeared, and the bears went hungry. What happened to the missing fish? Many scientists believe sea lice were to blame. Sea lice, tiny parasitic organisms that feed off the flesh of salmon and other fish, are natural in the ocean. Mature salmon are commonly found with a few sea lice on them. But in the concentrated environment of fish farms, sea lice can multiply to the point where there are so many that they become dangerous. Experts think wild salmon *smolts*—the name given to young salmon migrating to sea—in the Broughton Archipelago were infected by sea lice when their migration took them past fish farms. The young salmon were simply not strong enough to withstand the attacks by sea lice, and they died in huge numbers. That meant fewer young wild salmon were around to grow up. And fewer grown salmon in the ocean meant fewer fish

JUST THE BEAR FACTS

Why are grizzlies called grizzlies?
British Columbian grizzlies are close cousins of brown bears who live in Russia, so they could easily be called brown bears too. The reason North Americans called their brown bear "grizzly" is that its coat is "grizzled" with streaks of dark brown, silver and black fur. It has nothing to do with the word "grisly," which refers to something that inspires horror or fear in people. It just so happens that the words sound the same. Grizzly bears could just as easily have been called "stripy bears."

LEFT: **Bears love salmon eggs and sometimes are able to squeeze the body of the salmon so the eggs pop into their mouths like little candies. The eggs may be small but they're so full of fat that bears will choose them over all other parts of the salmon if they can.**

JUST THE BEAR FACTS

What would happen if the salmon did not return to spawn?

It's no exaggeration to say that salmon are the lifeblood of the rainforest. Without them there would be no great trees or great bears. So when salmon runs become extinct due to overfishing, pollution, fish farming or other causes, it's not just the salmon that disappear. The whole ecosystem begins to fall apart, and animals such as bears, whales, eagles, mink and river otters, all of whom rely on salmon, suffer.

returning to the rivers and streams to spawn and feed the bears. Instead bears living near the Broughton Archipelago had to rely on less-nourishing plant material to feed themselves for the long winter ahead.

Much the same thing happened farther north several years later when chum salmon failed to return to a number of rivers along the central BC coast. And because of that, all kinds of bears—grizzlies, blacks and spirit bears—starved to death. Before then it was common to see crowds of bears along rainforest riverbanks, feasting on the salmon that streamed in by the millions on their way home. But without the salmon there was nothing for the bears to feast on, so they went hungry. It was thought that overfishing by people was to blame.

In a good year, however, millions of chinook, chum, pink, coho and sockeye will fight their way up the many streams of the Great Bear Rainforest to spawn. But even in that good year, many won't succeed because of all the animals that catch and eat them on the way—animals like whales, seals, humans and bears. Because when it comes to salmon fishing, no one has tricks like a wily old bear.

When the salmon return to the rivers, bears from all over the forest put their hermit ways aside and gather together to fish. It's like a great big, months-long fishing derby, because to a bear there's nothing better than the season's first taste of salmon; to them it's like chocolate to a child. As usual, the biggest, strongest bears—usually the biggest, strongest grizzlies—get the best fishing spots. Weaker bears and mothers and cubs have to make do with places

where the pickings aren't as rich. But in the fall, if everything goes the way nature intends, there should be so many salmon that no one goes hungry.

Bears, like people, have different tastes, especially when it comes to eating salmon. Some like the fatty eggs best. Others like the skin and brains. Some aren't nearly as fussy and will eat the head, the tail and almost everything in between. What they don't eat they throw away. After a day of bear fishing, the rainforest's riverbanks stink to high heaven. The odor is so strong you might think you'd walked into a fish-packing plant by mistake. But not for long, because in the end not one scale is wasted. There's no such thing as garbage in the rainforest,

TOP: **These bears are taking an afternoon nap and a break from a hard morning's fishing. In the fall, bears consume so much salmon that they have to rest from time to time to digest their dinner. Sometimes the bears' bellies get so big they have to dig holes in the ground before they can lie down comfortably. These holes are called belly pits.**

Grizzly bears needn't think twice before swimming across a river or inlet. They are superb swimmers and can swim many kilometers of open ocean if necessary.

especially when it comes to salmon. Don't forget, it's probably fair to say that the whole rainforest lives in some way off the salmon's shiny backs. Even the trees benefit, because when the bears drag the salmon carcasses from the water, they leave what they don't eat on the ground. Then, thanks to all the microscopic creatures that feed on those carcasses, they decompose into the soil and fill it with nutrients. Think of it as nature's compost, because just like compost that feeds a vegetable garden, the good things that come from the salmon help the rainforest trees grow faster and taller. They also make for sweeter, tastier berry patches. So in a way, when bears haul salmon out of the river and drop them on the ground, they're like gardeners preparing beds for planting.

As any gardener will tell you, it's not unusual to use fish fertilizer to help plants grow. Now you know why.

Bears also have their own special fishing styles. Some will plunge headfirst into the water and grab fish in their jaws. A few show-offs will throw themselves belly-first into a stream, but as with a lot of show-offs, it's a losing strategy. Mostly their loud splashes scare the fish away. Others sit patiently on the river's edge, stick their paws in the water and scoop the fish out as if they were spooning corn flakes from a bowl. Some wait for the fish to leap out of the water so they can grab them in midair. Some pin the salmon against rocks with their long claws, while others jump on top of them and crush them between their front elbows and stomach. A couple of cagey individuals might stand in the water and do nothing. That way they fool the fish into mistaking their legs for protective tree trunks. Then when the salmon thinks it's found a safe hiding place, the bear strikes and gobbles it up. For the unlucky fish, it's the last mistake it'll ever make.

Some of the bears who turn up to fish are the rainforest's rare and precious white or Kermode bears—or as they're now known around the world, spirit bears. Spirit bears are only found on a few islands and the nearby mainland in the very heart of the Great Bear Rainforest, and in the whole world there are thought to be only about four hundred of them. In other words, only about one in every ten black bears found on these few islands is white. But even though they look different from black bears and are called by a different name, they are simply black bears

JUST THE BEAR FACTS

How do salmon spawn?

When salmon reach their spawning grounds, females dig a little depression in the gravel with their tails. As they release their eggs into this nest, male salmon will release a cloud of what is called *milt* over the eggs. It's this milt that contains the male salmon's sperm. Once the eggs are fertilized, the female will cover the nest with gravel and move on to dig a second nest where the whole process begins again. This occurs several times until the female has emptied herself of all her eggs. Then both the male and female stand guard over the nests until they die. The future of the salmon now lies buried in the gravel, ready to begin the cycle anew.

of a different color. They're the same size as regular black bears and often have black-furred parents and/or brothers and sisters. The only difference is they're white, though some have a slight marmalade tint to them. Sometimes when you see them on a misty gray day, they look more like ghosts than real flesh-and-blood bears.

Why are they white? That's another rainforest mystery. Some scientists think their pale color helps them fish better. It makes sense. Imagine you're a salmon looking up through the water at the gray sky. If a black bear is standing above you ready to pounce, you're going to notice it. But if the bear is the same color as the sky, you might not because the white bear's fur will blend into the gray. And if you can't see something, you're not going to hide from it. That would give the white or spirit bear a natural advantage over its black cousins—at least during the day.

JUST THE BEAR FACTS

Is the spirit bear related to the polar bear?

No. Even though they're both white, spirit bears are essentially black bears in everything except color. Polar bears are a separate species of bear. Polar bears are also much bigger than spirit bears. In fact, polar bears, which can grow to as much as 650 kilograms (1,450 pounds) in weight, are the largest bear species in the world. The biggest spirit bears grow to only about half that size, and most are much smaller.

LEFT: **Some scientists believe spirit bears are white because their lighter color helps them catch more salmon than their black cousins. They reckon their white fur blends in with the sky and this fools the salmon into thinking nothing is there.**

RIGHT: **A spirit bear snorkels for salmon.**

This is how evolution works. When an animal is born with a natural or biological advantage over its brothers and sisters and cousins, it becomes a stronger, more adaptable animal, and a stronger, more adaptable animal is more likely to breed than a weaker one. And when that stronger animal breeds, it will pass on its natural advantage to its offspring, so they'll be stronger too. Then when they breed, their children will have the same advantage to pass on to their children. And so on and so on. Maybe, scientists speculate, that's how the spirit bear got its white fur.

A First Nations legend tells a different story. It suggests that Raven, the creator of the rainforest and its resident trickster, flew among all the black bears and turned every tenth one white as a reminder of the last ice age, which ended about 12,000 years ago. This is as good an explanation as any because no one knows for sure. What do you think?

What is certain, however, is the special place spirit bears hold in the hearts and culture of native people along British Columbia's central coast. First Nations stories say that after turning the bears white, Raven promised them they would be the best bear fishers on the coast, and that they would live forever in peace and harmony in an eternally green rainforest. And until the coming of non-Native settlers to the BC coast, Raven's promise was kept.

The Tsimshian people have told the story of Moksgm'ol, their name for the spirit bear, for generations. But non-Native people only came to know of them in the early 1900s when settlers working

JUST THE BEAR FACTS

Where can you see a spirit bear?

You have to travel to a few remote islands in the Great Bear Rainforest—the only place in the world where they're found—and that isn't easy. Usually you have to go with someone who has a boat. There are no spirit bears in zoos, though beginning in 1924 a six-month-old orphaned female lived for twenty-four unhappy years in a cage in Victoria's Beacon Hill Park. She was captured by Francis Kermode from a man who was trying to smuggle her across the border to America. Her name was Ursus after her Latin name, *Ursus Kermodei.* Since then three orphaned spirit bear cubs have been captured, cared for and released back into the wild by wildlife rehabilitators. Three fully grown spirit bears—all of them killed illegally—have been stuffed and put on permanent display in the city of Terrace. One is in the Northwest Regional Airport, one is in the Chamber of Commerce office and one is in the council chamber at City Hall.

LEFT: **White mother bears can have black cubs and black mother bears can have white cubs in the Great Bear Rainforest. Sometimes sibling cubs are both black and white.**

JUST THE BEAR FACTS

Is the spirit bear genetically distinct from all other coastal bears?

Yes. According to research done cooperatively by a forest company, the BC government and the University of British Columbia, hair collected from a spirit bear was found to contain a single pair of genes that stopped whatever it is that turns a normal black bear's fur black. Instead the bear's fur was left a creamy white. This genetic marker or variant has never been found in any other mammal, proving that the spirit bear is indeed a genetically distinct animal.

RIGHT: **Grizzly bear with a fresh-caught pink salmon. On a good day's fishing, bears like this one can catch more than ten salmon every hour.**

in the region began to hear stories of a spirit bear haunting the forest. Occasionally a white pelt would turn up at fur trading posts, but even then the idea of a white bear was thought by most people to be fantastic. Some traders thought the pelts came from polar bears who had somehow lost their way and traveled south.

Now, more than a hundred years later, the spirit bear is anything but a secret. Thanks to the efforts of First Nations and environmentalists, the bear has become an international conservation symbol. But you can only find it in the Great Bear Rainforest. This is yet another reason why the forest itself is so important. If the forest the spirit bear lives in isn't saved, the spirit bear won't be saved either.

By late November it's time for bears of all colors— black, white and grizzled—to return to their dens or build new ones. By this time, if things have gone their way, their coats will be thick and shaggy, and their stomachs will be so full of fish—not to mention crab apples, angelica, cow parsnip and other plants that grow to their ripest and tastiest in fall—they'll drag on the ground. Some bears grow so fat they can no longer lie flat to sleep. First they have to dig a hole in the ground to fit their huge bellies. At this point they're more like seals than bears. They're also calmer and less aggressive than at any other time. No wonder. Have you ever heard the expression "fat and happy"? It applies to bears too. When that happens, they know it's been a good year.

JUST THE BEAR FACTS

When were spirit bears discovered?

First Nations people who live in the rainforest have always known about spirit bears. But it wasn't until about a hundred years ago that other people learned about them. In the early 1900s, a scientist named William T. Hornady, then the head of the New York Zoological Society, believed spirit bears represented a whole new species of bear. He hired Francis Kermode, the curator of the BC Natural History Museum in Victoria, to study the bear and bring one to New York. Kermode never did deliver a spirit bear to the US, but his name is still linked with them. Sometimes they're called *Kermode* bears. But while Francis's last name was pronounced *ker-**moad***, the bear's name is pronounced *ker-**mo**-dee*. Some people think it's because *ker-**moad*** sounds too much like *commode*, an old-fashioned word for toilet. And no one wanted to name such a splendid animal after a toilet.

RIGHT: **This spirit bear looks like he is practicing yoga but is only giving his itchy back a nice scratch. Due to their salmon diet, spirit bears on the coast can grow quite large, but they generally do not get much heavier than about 200 kilograms (450 pounds).**

CHAPTER SIX

Winter Again

As October turns into November, it's time for the bears of the Great Bear Rainforest to go to sleep again. Many will return to the same dens they used the previous winter. A few will build new ones. But after seven months of roaming around a vast rainforest, they will now spend the next five in a space not much bigger than the inside of a hollow tree. There will be just enough room for an adult bear to get up and turn around and perhaps for cubs to stretch their still-growing legs. But that's all the room they'll need, since they'll spend most of those five months snoozing and snoring.

Outside, winter will begin to take over the coast, and for a bear that means few opportunities for food. This is why bears evolved to spend the winter asleep. At the ocean's edge it will rain and hail

LEFT: **Winter covers the Great Bear Rainforest in a white blanket of snow. Long cold winters are rare in the temperate rainforest because the climate is moderated by the ocean, and the ocean stays a relatively constant temperature.**

JUST THE BEAR FACTS

What sounds do bears make?

This depends on the mood the bear is in. When bear cubs nurse, they produce a continuous motor-like purr almost like a cat's. Adults can make this sound too, only deeper and richer. Mother bears often "speak" to their cubs in a series of grunts, though what each of these grunts means is a secret kept by bears. Bears also blow air and clack their teeth when they're afraid. And if they're very afraid, they'll moan. Bear cubs will scream, almost like a human, when they're in distress, especially when they get separated from their mothers.

RIGHT: **When winter sets in, all rainforest bears should be safely tucked away in their high-elevation dens, ready to sleep away the long, dark and cold months ahead.**

and sleet. Occasionally it will get cold enough for snow. Then the ground will change from its usual brown and green to white, and the rainforest will be beautiful in a whole new way, like a scene on a Christmas card. It will be dark too. Towards the end of the year the days will be only a few hours long, and what little light there is will be faint, like a flame that's about to go out.

Bears build their dens up in the mountains, 300 meters (1,000 feet) high or higher, and up there it snows all winter long. Little by little, as November becomes December, and December becomes January, it deepens and deepens so that eventually the bears' dens will vanish under a thick carpet of white. Bears count on this deep layer of snow to keep their dens warm and private—like secret igloos buried under a rainforest.

When they enter their dens, rainforest bears are a third heavier than they were in spring. Their scrawn has turned to brawn thanks to the hundreds of delicious meals they enjoyed in the spring, summer and fall. All the plants and nuts and bugs and berries and, most of all, salmon they feasted on have made them fat. Good thing too, because they will live off this fat until March. In fact, they often won't eat another bite until spring.

But if you think winter is a dead time for bears, think again. Remember, winter is when bears are born. They mate in late spring or early summer, but it's in winter when mother bears, holed up in their dens under thick snowy blankets, give birth to their cubs. That's why winter is so hard on them. Not only do

they use up all the fat they stored feeding themselves, but they also have to use it to produce milk to feed their cubs. Normally bears have two cubs, but if they're weak or if the food supply the previous year was meager, they may have only one. On the other hand, if the salmon run was especially rich and the berries especially plentiful, they may have three or even, very occasionally, four. But even one cub requires a lot of milk to survive a winter.

But survive they will, on sleep and the promise of another spring. Next March when the snow outside their den doors melts and the rainforest plants start to grow, the bears of the Great Bear Rainforest will make their way into the world again, just as countless generations of bears have done before them. They've been the luckiest bears on Earth.

JUST THE BEAR FACTS

How do bears survive their long winter's sleep?

When bears go to sleep for the winter, they still need to eat. They do this by processing the reserves of fat they've built up during the months prior to hibernation. A sleeping bear can use up as many as 4,000 calories a day, or the equivalent of 11 fish burgers.

LEFT: **In just a few weeks this little cub, already wearing his winter coat, will join his mother and return to the den he was born in high above the forest's rivers.**

RIGHT: **Typical grizzly bear den excavated under the base of a western red cedar tree. Bears often choose to build their dens under the protection of an old tree like this one because it not only protects them from winter avalanches but also helps keep them dry in case it gets warm and rains.**

77

CHAPTER SEVEN

What the Future Might Hold

Can the bears of the Great Bear Rainforest survive? Only time will tell. Thanks to agreements negotiated among the British Columbia government, First Nations, industry and environmental groups, about thirty percent of the rainforest is now protected. However, the seventy percent that isn't protected remains open to logging and other kinds of industrial activity, although the government now says any work that does take place must be done in an environmentally friendly way.

The agreements are a start but by no means a solution. Scientists hired by the government to study the forest recommend that close to seventy percent of it be protected to ensure the long-term survival of its bears and other wildlife. Also, while carrying out industrial activity in a "more environmentally

LEFT: **This black bear may have had a white spirit-bear mother, and it might give birth to a white cub one day. Humans are just beginning to understand the complexities of the rainforest, including the question of why one out of every ten black bears on this part of the coast is pure white.**

JUST THE BEAR FACTS

How does the rainforest benefit us?

One of the most obvious ways is as a carbon sink. The release of carbon dioxide into the atmosphere is the source of global warming and climate change. When too much carbon dioxide gets released, it traps heat; that makes the whole world hotter. But plants, especially big plants like the trees in the Great Bear Rainforest, absorb carbon dioxide so it doesn't get into the atmosphere. The forest is also a great source of oxygen that humans and all animals, including bears, need to breathe. Have you ever heard people call the Amazon rainforest the Earth's lungs? That's because while we breathe oxygen in and carbon dioxide out, plants do the opposite. So when you have a great concentration of plants, like in the Amazon rainforest or the Great Bear Rainforest, they provide a ready and constant source of oxygen for people— and bears.

RIGHT: **Grizzly bears are extremely vulnerable to unnatural disturbances. This is why humans need to work hard to protect grizzly bear habitat and their food supply of salmon.**

friendly way" may sound like a good idea, no one has said what "more environmentally friendly" really means. Another problem is that the thirty percent of the forest set aside for protection is not the thirty percent where the bears and other animals live. Much of it is rock and ice, and many of the areas that have been protected are too small to support animals like the grizzly.

There are other worries too. Sport hunting of bears is still allowed in parts of the rainforest. This is especially bad for grizzly bears, who reproduce slowly. If one dies, it can take years before another bear is born to take its place. And even though more than three-quarters of all British Columbians are against sport hunting, the government refuses to end it.

Then there is the uncertainty about future salmon runs. Though the government has said no new salmon farms will be built in the northern part of the rainforest, they're still in the central and southern areas of the coast. As discussed earlier, salmon farms affect bears because they spread parasites that can kill wild salmon, the most important food rainforest bears have. Then there's overfishing. If too many wild salmon are caught by people, there won't be enough left to feed the rainforest. And if that wasn't enough, the federal government, along with the Alberta and British Columbia provincial governments, is proposing to build oil pipelines across western Canada that would end in the Great Bear Rainforest. This would open up the sensitive waters that protect the Great Bear to potentially catastrophic oil spills. In 1989, an oil tanker

Present vs. Historic Grizzly Bear Range

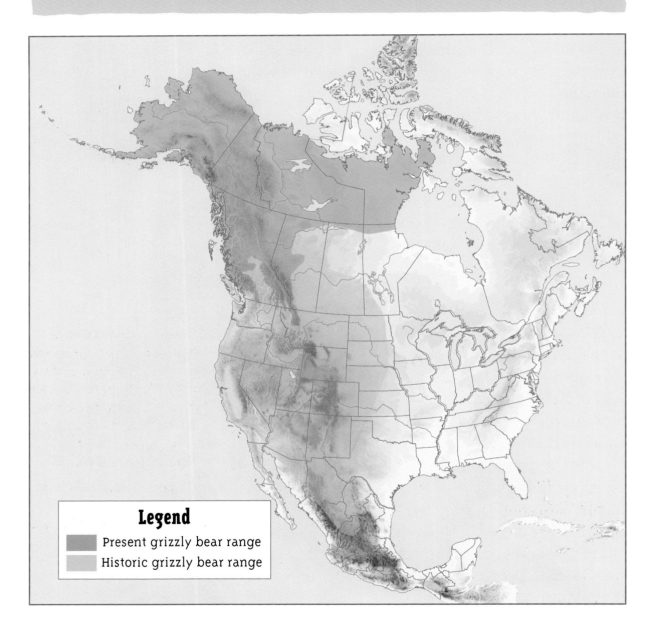

Legend
Present grizzly bear range
Historic grizzly bear range

named *Exxon Valdez* ran aground in Prince William Sound in Alaska and dumped almost 42 million liters (11 million gallons) of crude oil into the sea. This calamitous event killed tens of thousands of animals and required more than 11,000 people to clean it up. If an oil port was built in the Great Bear Rainforest, a disaster like that could happen there too.

Finally, there's climate change. Salmon are very sensitive to changes in ocean temperatures, which means if the ocean warms even a few degrees, the number of salmon could drop dramatically. The rivers could warm up too. And without the millions of salmon that swim the rivers and streams of the Great Bear Rainforest each fall, it may not be so great anymore.

The challenge that comes with saving a place like the Great Bear Rainforest is that people rarely look far into the future. Politicians only think ahead to the next election. Businesspeople want to make sure they earn more money this year than last. And ordinary people worry so much about putting food on the table and making sure their children are looked after they don't have time for much else. So when it comes to something like the fate of the Great Bear Rainforest, too often politicians and industrialists only see the short-term gain that comes from cutting down its trees, damming its rivers for electricity and opening up its inlets to oil tankers. And ordinary people doubt there's much they can do to stop it.

JUST THE BEAR FACTS

What effect does logging have on rainforest bears?

Logging can damage the rivers and creeks that spawning salmon depend on, and if there are fewer spawning salmon around, there will be less for bears to eat. The noise of logging in high-elevation areas can force bears out of their winter dens. In some cases, the very trees bears sleep under can be cut down. Roads built into the rainforest to enable timber trucks to take logs away can be used by hunters and poachers too, so it's much easier for them to get to the bears to kill them.

LEFT: **This map shows that, in North America, grizzly bears once roamed across the open prairies with the buffalo and far down into Mexico. Today they only survive in the relatively few remaining wilderness areas, mostly in northern Canada and Alaska.**

The Great Bear Rainforest is the most southerly stronghold for grizzly bears on the Pacific coast.

There's a lyric in a well-known pop song that goes "You don't know what you've got till it's gone." This means you don't always appreciate what you have in front of you until someone takes it away. The Great Bear Rainforest is so remote that we may not appreciate yet just what a treasure it is—one of the last truly great wildernesses in the world. It is every bit as rich and wondrous as Australia's Great Barrier Reef and Brazil's Amazon rainforest basin. But thanks to the hard work of conservationists and aboriginal people, that's starting to change. More and more people *are* starting to recognize its uniqueness. Before the early 1990s, no one had ever heard the words Great Bear Rainforest. Now it's an expression millions of people know. And every year more and more ordinary folk put more and more pressure on people in power to think past tomorrow and consider the many more tomorrows that come after that.

This is what will save the rainforest in the long run. As more people learn about it and come to care about all the varied and special animals in it, there's every chance that things will change, and the bears, wolves, deer and moose who call it home today will continue to call it home tomorrow and for years to come—living proudly and safely under its great green life-giving umbrella.

JUST THE BEAR FACTS

What else do bears eat?

Coastal bears have a long menu of food to choose from. In the spring they might get to eat a little oily fish called oolichan that swims to the rainforest rivers to spawn, or they might choose to eat clumps of tiny white herring eggs that cling to seaweed at low tide. A lucky bear might come across a beached whale or seal, and they have even been observed swimming out to little nesting islands to eat bird eggs. Not many bears have so many delicious choices!

LEFT: **Bears throughout the rainforest face an uncertain future because of habitat loss, trophy hunting and declining food supplies, such as wild salmon.**

FOR MORE INFORMATION

The bears of the Great Bear Rainforest need your help. Trophy hunting, diminishing salmon stocks, habitat loss and oil spills threaten these magnificent animals.

Pacific Wild is a non-profit wildlife conservation organization that is committed to protecting the bears in the Great Bear Rainforest by developing and implementing solution-based strategies that protect wildlife and their habitat. Pacific Wild has been at the forefront of large carnivore conservation on the British Columbia coast by supporting innovative research, public education, community outreach and awareness to achieve the goal of lasting wildlife protection. A portion of the royalties earned from the sale of this book will support Pacific Wild's work to protect bears in the Great Bear Rainforest.

For more information on Pacific Wild's conservation work or to learn more about the bears of the Great Bear Rainforest please contact:

Pacific Wild
PO Box 26
Denny Island, BC
V0T 1B0
Canada

WEBSITE: www.pacificwild.org
EMAIL: info@pacificwild.org

RESOURCES

Commercial Bear Viewing Association

The Commercial Bear Viewing Association of BC (CBVA) was formed to promote sustainable bear viewing in British Columbia and aid in the protection of wild bears and their ecosystems.

www.bearviewing.ca

OTHER SUGGESTED READING

McAllister, Ian. *Last Wild Wolves: Ghosts of the Rain Forest.* Vancouver: Greystone Books, 2007.

McAllister, Ian, Karen McAllister and Cameron Young. *The Great Bear Rainforest: Canada's Forgotten Coast.* Madeira Park: Harbour Publishing, 1997.

Russell, Charles. *Spirit Bear: Encounters with the White Bear of the Western Rainforest.* Toronto: Key Porter Books, 2002.

INDEX

Page numbers in **bold** refer to photographs.

IAN McALLISTER is a founding director of Pacific Wild, a Canadian non-profit wildlife conservation group. An award-winning author and photographer, he has spent more than twenty years working to protect the West Coast's temperate rainforest. Ian lives with his family on an island in the heart of the Great Bear Rainforest.

NICHOLAS READ, a lifelong lover of animals, works as a journalism instructor at Langara College in Vancouver, British Columbia. He has written for the *Vancouver Sun, The Globe and Mail, Toronto Star* and other publications and authored two prize-winning children's books.

ABOUT THE ARTIST

An artist from childhood, Martin Campbell's work reflects scenes of his daily life and Heiltsuk culture. "I have been lucky to spend years of my life down at Kvai River watching grizzly bears at my doorstep. I understand why the grizzly bear is an important symbol in Heiltsuk society."